My Little Book of
Cats and
Kittens

by David Alderton

Sandy Creek
NEW YORK

Sandy Creek
NEW YORK

An Imprint of Sterling Publishing Co., Inc.
1166 Avenue of the Americas
New York, NY 10036

SANDY CREEK and the distinctive Sandy Creek logo
are registered trademarks of Barnes & Noble, Inc.

Text © 2016 by QEB Publishing, Inc.
Illustrations © 2016 by QEB Publishing, Inc.

ISBN 978-1-4351-6413-0

Manufactured in Guangdong, China
Lot #:
2 4 6 8 10 9 7 5 3 1
06/16

www.sterlingpublishing.com

Words in **bold**
are explained
in the glossary
on page 60.

Contents

Introduction

Cats are among the most popular animals to keep as pets. They have been keeping people company for nearly 10,000 years.

>> Cats love to play! It helps them to find out about the world.

<< In the wild, cats are hunters. Their bodies and teeth are suited to catching birds and mice.

Cats are separated into different **breeds**. Each breed has a special look and way of behaving. Some cats are bred to look like wild cats. Others may be bred for their curly hair or short legs.

⌄ All cats lick their coats to clean themselves.

5

American Bobtail

The American bobtail is named for its short tail—it's only about one-third the length of most cats' tails.

˅ Bobtails have a sweet, kind nature.

˄ These loving cats like to watch their owners.

The first American bobtail was a kitten named Yodi. He was found in Arizona about 50 years ago. This cat's kittens also had bobtails.

⌃ The tufts of fur on a bobtail's ears and toes make it look a little wild.

American Curl

The first thing you notice about this cat is its strange ears—they curl backward!

« The kittens are born with straight ears. The ears curl after about 10 days.

⌄ **American curls love people and like to watch what they are doing.**

The first American curl was a **stray** kitten named Shulamith. She moved in with a couple in California in 1981. The breed started when her kittens had curly ears, too.

⌃ **This alert cat's ears face forward, but the tips of its ears curl backward.**

9

American Shorthair

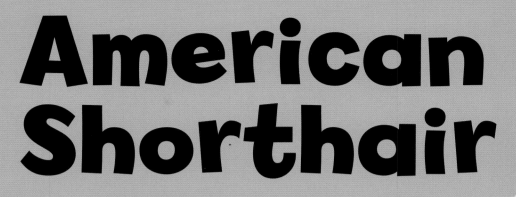

The American shorthair came to America aboard ships of explorers and settlers. It is a stocky cat with strong muscles.

« **This kitten has a silver tabby coat.**

American shorthairs come in a wide range of colors and patterns. Tabby markings are most common.

>> This cat enjoys playtime. It is also good at hunting.

⌃ American shorthairs are friendly and like to sit next to their owners.

Bengal

The Bengal has beautiful markings—it looks like a little **leopard**. The first Bengals were the kittens of a wild Asian leopard cat and a **domestic cat**.

⌄ **This cat loves to roll on its back and purr when someone strokes it.**

« **Bengal kittens can be full of fun and very lively.**

Bengals love to run and tumble. They can leap great heights and climb doors and cupboards. They also enjoy trying to catch the drops from a dripping faucet.

⌃ The Bengal is smart and can be trained to wear a leash.

Bombay

The Bombay has black, glossy fur. It was bred to look like a miniature black **panther**.

⌄ The Bombay is playful and can be taught to play games of fetch.

⌄ Bombays in the United States have gold- or copper-colored eyes.

The Bombay loves its food. It may try to take it from the package before you can get it into the bowl!

∧ **This easy-going cat loves people and often gets along with dogs.**

British Longhair

This breed makes an excellent pet. It is friendly and loving, and likes to snuggle up with its family.

« British longhairs come in a wide range of colors and patterns.

The British longhair is a gentle, relaxed cat. It is also vocal and makes a range of different noises.

« This cat's soft, thick coat needs to be brushed several times a week.

⌃ These cats are usually calm, but they can have hyper moments!

British Shorthair

The British shorthair is bigger than most pet cats. This chunky cat looks as if it is smiling.

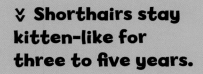 ⋁ Shorthairs stay kitten-like for three to five years.

18

The British shorthair came to Britain more than 2,000 years ago. It was brought by the **Romans**. It is smart and friendly, and comes in almost every color a cat can be.

⌃ **These playful cats are good at remembering tricks.**

« **The hairs of this cat's coat are short and dense—they grow close together.**

Burmese

The mother of the first Burmese kittens was born in Asia. She was a little brown cat with yellow eyes.

⌄ The kitten on the left is cream and the one on the right is lilac.

⌃ Burmese cats love people and can learn to play fetch and tag.

Today, Burmese cats come in a range of colors from rich brown to beige to cream.

∧ These cats are very friendly, even to strangers. They love to be stroked.

California Spangled

This spotted cat was bred to look and walk like a small leopard. It is a **rare breed**—there are only about 200 worldwide.

˅ Spangles love to watch what their owners are doing.

« The spangle walks with its body and tail held low, like a leopard.

These cats were bred to remind people how important it is to keep leopards safe. In the wild, some leopards are threatened.

>> Spangles have large whisker pads—the parts of the face their whiskers grow from.

European Shorthair

This cat was bred in Sweden from ordinary house cats. It is strong, friendly, and good at catching mice.

≪ Some European shorthairs like to snuggle up with their owners.

⌄ Some prefer to live outdoors. They like to have lots of space.

This cat usually gets along with other pets in its home, including dogs. It also lives happily with children.

>> Shorthairs come in lots of colors. This kitten has a tabby coat.

Highlander

This giant cat is a new breed—it was only started in 2004. It was bred to look like a **lynx**, which is a type of **big cat**.

↟ Some Highlanders have bobtails and slightly curled ears.

« These cats are gentle and friendly and enjoy playing hide-and-go-seek.

26

Highlanders are very smart cats. They can be taught to sit, fetch, and walk on a leash.

>> This cat loves to play and has lots of energy.

LaPerm

This unusual-looking cat has a curly coat and curly whiskers. The first LaPerm lived on a farm in Oregon in 1982.

⋁ This is a long-haired LaPerm. Some have short hair.

⋀ LaPerms are smaller than many breeds of cat.

>> Some kittens are born curly. Others go curly as they get older.

Some people call these cats "clowns," because they love attention. They may even tap their owners on their shoulders if they want something.

Maine Coon

This cat is very big and has a personality to match. The Maine coon is friendly, loving, and gentle, and is the most popular cat breed in the world.

>> Males grow bigger than the females.

<< These cats greet their owners with a trilling noise rather than a meow.

>> Maine coon kittens love to play games of catch and fetch.

Maine coons were the first cats to be bred in the United States. During the 1800s they were kept as farm cats to help catch mice.

Manx

This cat has no tail!
It comes from the Isle of
Man, an island off the
northwest coast of England.

ᐯ Manx kittens grow slowly.
They only reach full size when
they are about five years old.

The Manx breed dates to about 1750. The cats come in many colors. They often have a large amount of white on their coats.

^ These cats make good guard cats. They will growl if they hear a strange noise.

Munchkin

This cat is named for the Munchkin characters in the film *The Wizard of Oz.* Like the characters, this cat has very short legs.

⌃ A Munchkin's front legs are only about 3 inches long.

« These cats are smart and confident and like to have a lot of toys to play with.

When it wants to see something better, this cat sometimes sits up on its back legs, like a kangaroo.

« It is good at figuring out how to reach things that bigger cats can get at easily.

Norwegian Forest Cat

This large, handsome cat was bred to survive Norway's cold winters. It has a thick, **waterproof** coat to keep it warm outdoors.

« In winter, this cat has a thick **ruff** of extra-long fur on its chest.

In spring, it **sheds** its thick fur and loses its ruff. The "Wegie," short for "Norwegian," is a smart, energetic cat. It loves to roam outdoors, but also makes a great pet.

⌃ Tabby is a common coat pattern for this cat.

37

Ocicat

This striking cat was bred to look like a type of wild cat called an **ocelot**. Ocelots live in parts of Central and South America.

« The ocicat loves to play. This smart cat quickly learns new tricks.

⌄ This cat is medium to large in size. It does not like to be left on its own.

Ocicats and ocelots both have spotted coats, but ocicats are not at all wild—they make very loving pets. They will even ride on their owners' shoulders.

^ **The ocicat has an M-shaped marking above its eyes.**

Persian

The Persian's long, soft coat and large eyes make it a real glamor puss! It is also a devoted pet.

« This cat has a flat nose level with its eyes.

The Persian has a sweet nature. It is a quiet cat with a soft voice. It is not very active and usually prefers to live indoors.

⌄ **The Persian's coat needs to be brushed every day to keep it from getting matted.**

Russian blue

This shy, gentle cat was bred in the far north of Russia. It was taken to England and other European countries from the Russian port of Archangel in the 1860s.

« This gray coat color is known as **blue**.

» The Russian blue has a short, dense, silky coat.

At first it was known as the Archangel cat, but it was renamed the Russian blue because of its "blue" coat.

∧ This cat's eyes start off yellow but turn green after about four months.

43

Savannah

This adventurous cat is named for the plains of Africa. One of the parents of the first Savannah kitten was a type of African wild cat called a **serval**.

<< This cat has large ears like the serval. Its eyes are hooded.

The Savannah is alert and active. It can leap to great heights. It can also switch on a faucet and open a cupboard door!

<< The Savannah likes to explore and hunt for small animals.

Selkirk Rex

Cats with "rex" in their names have curly coats. The mother of the first Selkirk Rex kittens was a curly-coated cat found in a **rescue shelter** in Montana in 1987.

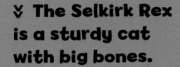

⌄ The Selkirk Rex is a sturdy cat with big bones.

» This cat is patient, loving, and laid-back. It likes to be cuddled.

∧ **The Selkirk Rex can have short hair, like the kitten on the left, or long hair.**

This cat's woolly curls can look quite scruffy. It's a good idea to comb them twice a week to get rid of any tangles.

Siamese

This beautiful, sleek cat is very graceful. It is also noisy and has a big personality.

⌄ The dark areas of fur—the feet, face, ears, and tail—are called **points.**

« Siamese kittens are born white, but parts of them get darker as they grow.

>> The Siamese loves to be kept busy with toys.

This cat leaps and dances like a ballerina. It also talks a lot and makes lots of different noises.

Siberian

This ancient breed of cat comes from Russia, where the winters are freezing cold for months on end. It needed its long, waterproof coat to survive there.

« The Siberian has a handsome, bushy tail.

Siberian cats are cheerful, loving, and loyal. Like a dog, a Siberian will run to greet its owner and may try to join in any activities it sees.

≪ **This cat's coat becomes thicker and longer in winter.**

⌃ **Siberian kittens grow quickly. They reach adult size after about 18 months.**

Somali

Somalis are full of curiosity. They want to find out about everything around them.

<< **The Somali will demand that you pay attention to it.**

You have to keep on your toes if you have a Somali. This cat loves to run and can be taught to play fetch and tag.

˅ **This cat loves to watch its owner from the highest place in the room.**

˄ **The hairs of a Somali's coat are shaded in dark and light bands.**

Sphynx

Have you ever seen a
bald cat? You have now!
In fact the Sphynx has some
hair on its body, but not much.

⌄ **This wide-eyed cat is one
of the friendliest breeds.
It loves attention.**

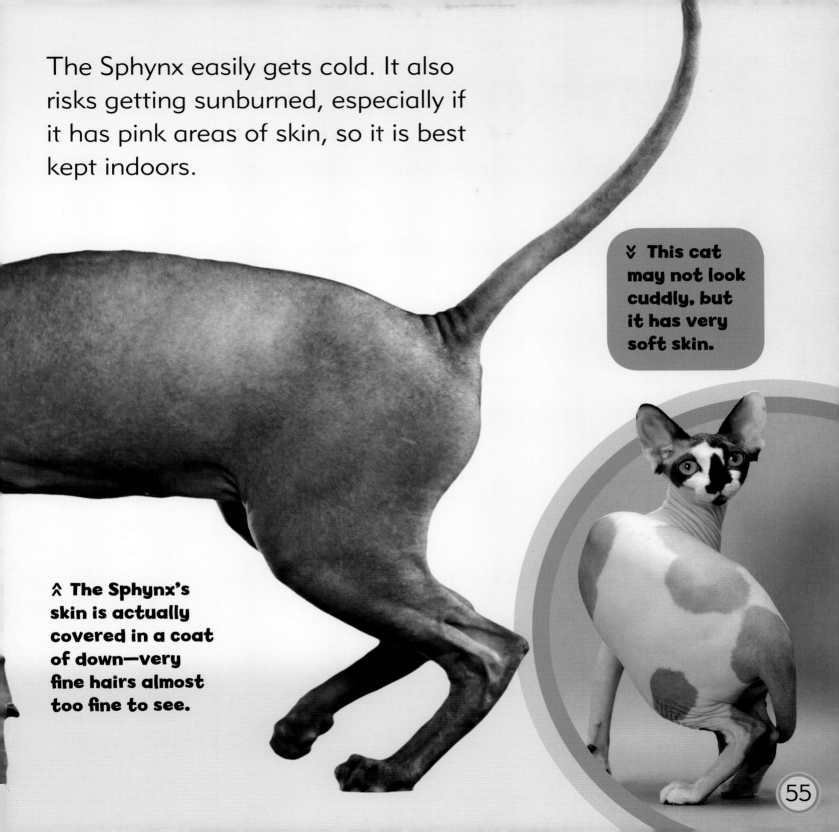

The Sphynx easily gets cold. It also risks getting sunburned, especially if it has pink areas of skin, so it is best kept indoors.

⌄ This cat may not look cuddly, but it has very soft skin.

⌃ The Sphynx's skin is actually covered in a coat of down—very fine hairs almost too fine to see.

Tonkinese

The first Tonkinese, or Tonk, had Burmese and Siamese parents. This breed has a pale body, often with a darker face and feet.

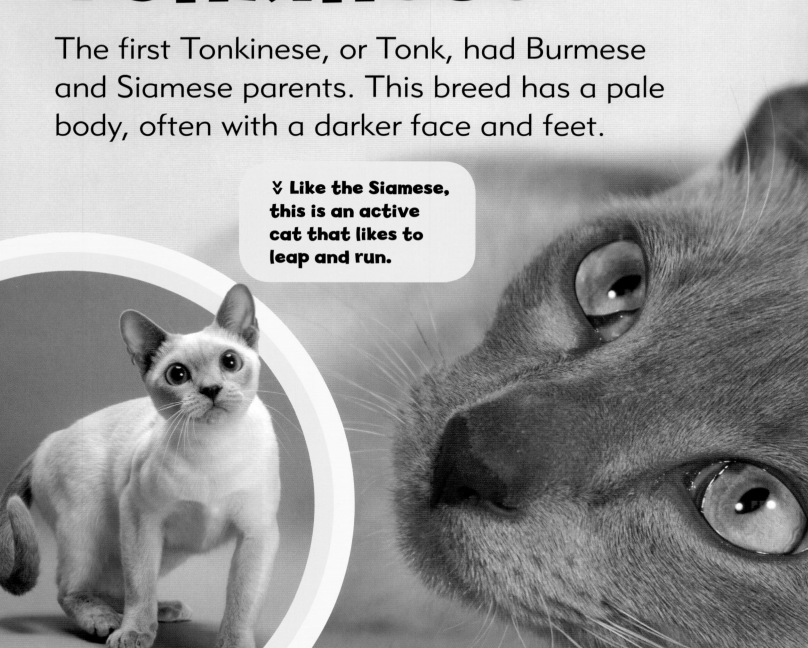

⩔ Like the Siamese, this is an active cat that likes to leap and run.

You can tell a Tonk from a Siamese because it has a rounder head. It is more likely to sit on its owner's lap than a Siamese.

⌄ Tonks have curved mouths that look as if they are smiling.

« Tonks are very loving. They like to be given lots of attention.

Turkish Angora

This breed has been kept in the area of Angora, Turkey, for thousands of years. It is the silkiest of all cats.

≪ The Turkish Angora has long ears, a bit like a rabbit, and a bushy tail.

>> **Turkish Angoras are often white.**

It is a strong, smart, and graceful cat that loves to play. The Turkish Angora may walk along curtain rails, or have fun pushing things off tabletops.

Glossary

big cat The name given to the four biggest wild cats—lions, tigers, jaguars, and leopards.

blue A gray coat color.

breed A particular type of cat or other animal. Animals that belong to a particular breed look similar.

dense Close together.

domestic cat A cat that is kept indoors as a pet—the opposite of a wild cat.

leopard A big cat with a brown coat and black markings. It lives in Asia and Africa, and likes to swim and climb trees.

lilac A pale pinkish-gray coat color.

lynx A wild cat with a short tail and ear tufts. Lynx live in North America, Europe, and Asia.

matted Tangled into a lump.

ocelot A medium-sized wild cat with a spotted coat, from Central and South America.

panther Another name for a leopard, especially one with black fur.

points The dark parts—such as the face, ears, feet, and tail—on a pale coat.

rare breed A breed that is rare outside the area it first came from.

rescue shelter A place where stray animals are fed and given shelter until a home can be found for them.

Romans The Romans were based in the city of Rome, in Italy. About 2,000 years ago they ruled an empire that stretched across Europe.

ruff The long hairs around the neck of a cat.

serval An African wild cat with long legs.

shed When hair naturally falls out.

stray A pet that no longer has a home.

tabby A gray or brown coat with dark stripes.

waterproof Stops water from getting through.

whisker pad A cat's whiskers grow from whisker pads. The pads are full of nerves that make the whiskers sensitive.

Index

lynx 26

M

Maine Coon 30, 31
Manx 32, 33
mice, catching 4, 24, 31
Munchkin 34, 35

N

Norwegian forest cat 36, 37

O

ocelots 38, 39
ocicat 38, 39

P

Persian 40, 41
play 4, 11, 14, 20, 26, 27,
    31, 35, 38, 49, 53, 59

R

rare breeds 22

Russian blue 42, 43

S

Savannah 44, 45
Selkirk Rex 46, 47
serval 44
Siamese 48, 49
Siberian 50, 51
Somali 52, 53
Sphynx 54, 55

T

tabby 10, 11, 25, 37
Tonkinese 56, 57
training 13, 14, 20, 27, 53
tricks 19, 38
Turkish Angora 58, 59

W

waterproof coats 36, 50
wild cats 4, 5, 12, 44

Picture credits